Mark A. Russo, CISSP-ISSAP

The National Institute of Standards and Technology (NIST) special publication series tells you "what to do." This supplement is designed to help you understand "how to" successfully implement the new US federal government cybersecurity contracting requirements.

Writing an Effective Plan of Action & Milestones (POAM)
Second Edition

FORWARD

This is an updated supplement regarding the Plan of Action and Milestone (POAM) thought-process and application. It is updated to better assist the novice through advanced cybersecurity professional address the recent changes in federal cybersecurity contracting requirements impacting companies doing business with the US federal government. The effort is designed to increase the cybersecurity posture of not only the federal government, but any business collecting, processing or disseminating sensitive information. It is designed to align with the groundbreaking 2018 cybersecurity book: *"DOD NIST 800-171 Compliance Guidebook."* The objective is to provide complete how-to guidance and instruction to effectively and quickly address business needs to secure their Information Technology (IT) environments, and to effectively compete in the federal contract space.

This is designed to be a workbook and template combination, but much like the *"Compliance Guidebook,"* is designed to lead businesses and their Information Technology (IT) staffs to better apply cybersecurity best practices. "It's about making the cryptic, comfortable" ™. These are plain-English solutions to the challenges of new and expanding Federal Government cybersecurity contract requirements.

Best to you,

Syber Risk LLC Team

LEGAL STUFF

Writing an Effective Plan of Action & Milestones (POAM)

Contents

Purpose

The **Plan of Action and Milestones (POAM)** is probably the least understood, but most vital component of the National Institute of Standards and Technology's **Risk Management Framework (RMF).** As such, this book is written based upon the RMF standards and guidelines that can be applied to 2016 released **National** Institute of Standards and Technology (NIST) Special Publication (SP) 800-171, revision 1, *Protecting Controlled Unclassified Information in Nonfederal Information Systems and Organizations, NIST 800-53 revision 4, Recommended Security Controls for Federal Information Systems and Organizations, and the National Cybersecurity Framework (NCF).* The derivative security controls are described in the respective frameworks mentioned and will help businesses and cybersecurity professionals prepare effective and complete POAMs.

This book also addresses compliance with the US Government's Federal Acquisition Regulation (FAR) clause 52.204-21 that and its companion DOD supplement, the Defense Federal Acquisition Regulation Supplement (DFARS), and its specific clause, 252.204-7012 that mandates companies conducting business with the government must be fully compliant.

A POAM is exactly what it is as described. It is a **plan**, specific to the selected security controls that cannot be adequately addressed. POAMs are also used to address vulnerabilities identified by security tools that assess the cybersecurity posture of an Information System (IS), and the associated plan to fix them. For the purposes of a NIST-based cybersecurity framework, it is typically applicable to the local physical and virtual network infrastructure that provides the "backbone" processes for a company to conduct business. Further, a POAM requires **milestones**. These are benchmark points in time that a company is expected to work to change a **non-compliant** control to a **compliant** status. Milestones are interim efforts that are managed by the IT staff and with corporate officer oversight to ensure an active risk management effort occurs.

While POAM preparation to many appears to be a challenging concept for even major businesses and contractors, this book is designed to define and break-down the process to assist business owners create both an effective and complete POAM. The objective is to submit a good-faith and accurate accounting of the respective IT environment. The cybersecurity posture will most likely be reported to a potential Contract Office or its designated oversight representative.

A POAM document is a key document in a System Security Plan (SSP). The overall collection of required documents is called a Security Authorization Package (SAP). For the purposes of this book, the SSP is a key artifact—and, we will refer to it as the primary document of-record. The POAM describes the specific tasks the business or agency has planned to correct any weaknesses or deficiencies in the security controls noted during an assessment and to address the residual vulnerabilities in the IS. Companies develop a POAM document typically using a **POAM Template** which will be presented as part of this instructional book. It will require businesses and their IT staff's compliance with security control requirements that are described as part of this "how-to" book. (This template is currently available online at https://cybersentinel.tech).

Additionally, the scope of a POAM includes security control executions (including all management, operational, and technical controls and their implementation) that have unacceptable deficiencies. This book is further intended to provide the business and its IT staff the ability to effectively develop, create, and manage their POAMs not just to meet the NIST-based framework requirements, but to provide a needed context to track and manage its own sensitive data from future loss, compromise or destruction.

The POAM provides a disciplined and structured method to reduce, manage, mitigate, and ultimately, address an active POAM finding/vulnerability. POAM's provide findings, recommendations, and actions that will correct the deficiency or vulnerability; it is not just identifying the risk but having a "plan" that reduces the dangers to *subjective* determination, by the System Owner (business), that the control is met.

Risk	Threat
Definition	Definition
A measure of the extent to which an entity is threatened by a potential circumstance or event, and typically a function of: (i) the adverse impacts that would arise if the circumstance or event occurs; and (ii) the likelihood of occurrence. Information system-related security risks are those risks that arise from the loss of confidentiality, integrity, or availability of information or information systems and reflect the potential adverse impacts to organizational operations (including mission, functions, image, or reputation), organizational assets, individuals, other organizations, and the Nation.	Any circumstance or event with the potential to adversely impact organizational operations (including mission, functions, image, or reputation), organizational assets, individuals, other organizations, or the Nation through an information system via unauthorized access, destruction, disclosure, modification of information, and/or denial of service.

Risk & Risk Management

A POAM captures the overall managed *risk*. Many confuse risk with **threat** and use the terms interchangeably. A threat, be it an intentional threat such as a hacker, or natural disaster, is a subset of risk. The standard cybersecurity equation for **risk** can be computed as following:

$$\text{RISK} = \text{Threat} \ \times \ \text{Vulnerability} \ \times \ \text{Consequence}$$

Furthermore, the POAM is a key tool to manage the risk over the life of the systems operational existence. The Risk Management Framework (RMF) created by NIST is based on active knowledge, recognition, and a plan to address by the business or agency to provide a reportable and repeatable mechanism that creates the real success of the concept of "risk management." This is not "risk elimination;" it's about an active means to manage risk, and any associated threats over time.

The Three Elements of Risk

The POAM is used to monitor progress in correcting weaknesses or deficiencies noted during the businesses own self-assessment and that "security control assessment" supports a continuous monitoring process. (See Appendix D for a more detailed discussion of "Continuous Monitoring".)

The POAM identifies:

- **The tasks (initial milestones) that need to be accomplished with a recommendation for completion that occur AFTER the IS's implementation.**

- **The scheduled completion dates the company has set for the POAM actions to be completed; this should be typically no more than one-year, with possibility of extension as agreed to between the business and the Contract Office.**

CRITICAL NOTE ABOUT POAM SECURITY:

How important is it to protect your POAM? It is EXTREMELY critical that your vulnerabilities are controlled and only released to personnel who require access to the information. If the POAM listing were to become public, would-be hackers would have an easy "blueprint" of how to exploit the IT infrastructure. POAM information should always be treated as highly sensitive and the sharing of it should only be with those with a clear need-to-know. Always treat POAM information as information that should be secured in at least lockable and restricted areas both in its hard copy as well as softcopy online form.

Body of Evidence

There are numerous available security controls from within the varied NIST frameworks. These controls are at the core of every POAM response. It is vital to understand that not all controls require a technologic solution. Personnel and procedure solutions may just as well meet the requirements of a control. The control should trace directly to the POAM with one or more mitigation efforts based upon the interpreted risk.

The **People, Process, and Technology (PPT) Model** is the recommended guidance for answering many of the controls within a POAM narrative. While solutions will not necessarily require a **technological** answer, consideration of the **people** (e.g., who? what skill sets? etc.) and **process** (e.g., notifications to senior management, action workflows, etc.) will meet many of the response requirements. The best responses will typically include the types and kinds of people assigned to oversee the control, the processes or procedures that identify the workflow that will ensure that the control is met, and in many cases, the technology that will answer the control in part or in full.

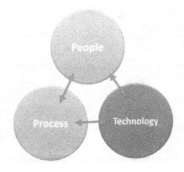

The PPT Model

On the next page is a basic workflow of the process from security control to POAM and System Security Plan (SSP). The traceability occurs from the specific security control, in this case, "apply whitelisting and blacklisting." From this point, the developer and system owner should determine whether the security control can be met, and how best to demonstrate it. This may include technical solutions that can be shown to a cybersecurity assessor in the form of a "screen capture" or actual view of onscreen policy settings or configurations readily demonstrable to an assessor. This could also be shown via documentation such as User Guides, System Administrators manuals, or Standard Operating Procedures (POC) that clearly articulate the alignment to the control; the assessor has three main means to assess completeness of a security control either through: 1) examination (which may include documentation); testing (actually observing a sequence of events that demonstrate a control is met) or 3) through interviews (of individuals such as system administrators, developer engineers, or the system owner).

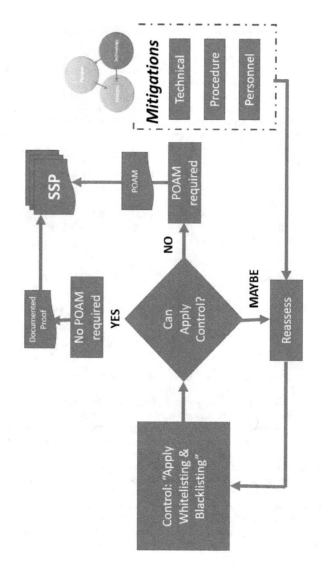

Basic POAM Work Flow Model (2018)

The first question that needs to be asked is whether "can [the system developer] apply [the] control"? There are only two answers: yes or no. Either the control can be met in full based upon a clear understanding of what the control requires or not. If the answer is "no" then a POAM needs to be developed that addresses "mitigating" factors. These, as described above using the PPT model, culminate to adequately or completely meeting the control; if there is no clear direction from the organization's cybersecurity Risk Management governance body, then it becomes a subjective determination of completeness. The subjectivity may be a determination by the company or organization where self-assessment is allowed[1], or by a "negotiation" with third-party assessors provide an audit of the system[2].

All information is captured in the SSP. The SSP is the collective cybersecurity state of the respective IT system. It is a dynamic collection of information that should be updated regularly. It forms the Body of Evidence (BOE) critical to a determination internally and externally that the system is "secure" and may be connected to another live system or the Internet in general.

---

[1] This may include NIST 800-171 or the National Cybersecurity Framework.
[2] More typical of NIST 800-53.

Proof of Cybersecurity Posture: The Body of Evidence

The basis of any NIST-framework is that developers, contractors, etc., provide adequate security on all Information Systems (IS). Typically, the minimum requirement to demonstrate control implementation is through **documentation**. Another term that is used is an **artifact**. An artifact is any representation to an independent third-party assessor that clearly shows compliance with a specific security control. It is a major part of the proof that a business owner would provide to DOD or other federal government contract offices.

The common term for the collection of all applicable and supporting artifacts is the Body of Evidence (BOE). The major items required for the BOE includes three major items:

1. **System Security Plan (SSP).** This is a standard cybersecurity document. It describes the company's overall IT infrastructure to include hardware and software lists. Where appropriate, suggestions of additional artifacts that should be included in this document and duplicated into a standard SSP format will be recommended. The current generalized direction for the SSP is the current minimum requirement for an artifact and must also include all Plans of Actions and Milestones (POAM).

2. **Company Policy** or **Procedure**. Any corporate direction provided to internal employees, subcontractors, and some third-party service providers such as Managed or Cloud Service Providers. This direction is typically enforceable under United States labor laws and Human Resource (HR) direction. It is recommended that such a policy or procedure artifact be a *singular* collection of how the company addresses each of the security controls.

3. **Plan of Action and Milestones (POAM).** This describes any control that the company cannot fix or fully demonstrate its full compliance. It provides an opportunity for a company to delay addressing a difficult to implement technical solution or in many cases may be cost-prohibitive.

   POAMs should always have an expected completion date and defined interim milestones (typically monthly) that describe the actions leading to a full resolution or implementation of the control. ***POAMs should not be for more than a year, however, a critical hint, a company may request an <u>extension</u> multiple times if unable to fully meet the control.***

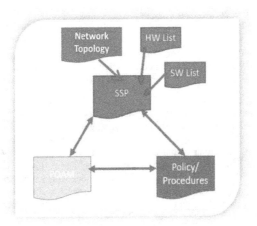

The Major Artifacts Required for NIST-based ATO packet

A POAM is a Living-Document;
you cannot just do it once and put it "on a shelf"

Active Management of Security Controls is intended to protect
your vital and sensitive data from
loss, compromise or destruction

The Role of Tailoring

For example, the 2016 version update to NIST 800-171, revision 1, provides a less than complete direction on the matter of **control tailoring**. It states in Appendix E that there are three primary criteria for the removal of a security control (or control enhancement):

> • **The control is uniquely federal (i.e., primarily the responsibility of the federal government):** The government directly provides the control to the company. While possible, expect this to not typically occur.

> • **The control is not directly related to protecting the confidentiality of CUI/CDI:** This will also not apply since all these controls were originally chosen to protect

the confidentiality of all CUI/CDI. That's why this book exists to better explain how to address these controls which are for the most part all required.

• **The control is expected to be routinely satisfied by Nonfederal Organizations (NFO) without specification:** In other words, the control is expected to be met by the NFO, i.e., the company. That is, you and your IT team.

Tailoring is completely allowed and recommended where appropriate. Within the NIST cybersecurity frameworks the concept of **tailoring-out** of a control is desirable where technically or operationally it cannot be reasonably applied. This will require technical certainty that the control is Non-Applicable (N/A). Under this opportunity, if the company's IT architecture does not contain within its **security boundary** the technology where such a control would be required to be applied then the control is identified as N/A.

For example, where the business has no Wi-Fi network in its security boundary, it can advise the government that any controls addressing the security of its Wi-Fi would be a N/A control. The business cannot nor have reason to implement this control because it currently doesn't allow Wi-Fi networks or any presence of such equipment such as Wi-Fi routers, antennas, etc. The control would be marked as **compliant** and annotated as N/A at the time of the self-assessment. It would still be required to identify that Wi-fi is not currently authorized in the company's cybersecurity procedure guide or policy.

When working with the government simple and consistent always helps through a very young and less-than-defined process

---

Courses of Action...Out of time

If you have purchased this book, you are looking for answers, and you are looking for them quickly. *How can my company meet the numerous NIST security controls?* What are the challenges? What are the costs in terms of both time and money? There are **four** likely courses of action:

- **OPTION 1: Hire an outside agency** that can assemble the information needed and prepare all documents required. Typically, at a cost of thousands of dollars.

- **OPTION 2: Use internal IT and cybersecurity expertise** to assemble and prepare the required documents and address all the controls completely to meet an internal deadline or a deadline from a prime contractor. This is most likely based on an urgency from the prime and needs to be addressed quickly or lose business because the business cannot satisfy all NIST control requirements.

- **OPTION 3: Attempt a good-faith effort** using available NIST publications and resources that only describe "what" is required, but not the "how" to do it. Assemble the System Security Plan (SSP), the Corporate Cybersecurity Policy document, and the Plans of Action and Milestones. Attempt a partial action to satisfy the NIST controls.

- **OPTION 4: POAM everything; it is an acceptable solution.** There is no time to do anything substantial. POAM all controls with a planned completion of no later than one year from submission.

Option 1 is available to the business and it may be worth the cost. If the business does not have the resident expertise, Option 1 may be its only recourse. Private companies in this area are charging $1500-$3000 for typical services to prepare the BOE.

Option 2 considers the company has a good foundational team that can handle the security control requirements. It understands its current IT environment and can confidently describe and document it in the SSP, Company Policy, and POAM document. This effort is not expected to be complete. There will be controls that cannot be technically or financially met to address current Security Authorization Package timelines. It too should be considered a good-faith effort that is intended to describe in adequate detail the nature of security within the business's respective IT network security boundary.

Option 3 assumes minimal capabilities to meet the NIST controls. This could include limited IT or cybersecurity expertise and may require some outside consulting support as needed. The book, **"NIST 800-171: Beyond DOD"**, is designed best to help in this area; currently available on Amazon. This is a good-faith effort and expects that most of controls will require a POAM. There is **nothing** wrong with having POAMs. The real issue occurs when a company or agency does not actively manage them; this is what "risk management" is designed to truly accomplish.

Option 4 is essentially that there is no time. The Contract Officer or prime contractor has directed that your company comply. The quickest (and least recommended solution) is to POAM all controls. Those controls that can be addressed purely with documentation may take several months. More technical controls may take even longer. The solution is to populate the POAM template (this template is currently available at https://cybersentinel.tech) with all controls and select dates from 30 days to 365 days as expected completion dates for the POAMs resolution. *Don't make them all one year; that shows desperation, but worse, a lack of resource planning that will eventually damage the company's effort and credibility.*

There are several ways to effectively meet the POAM requirement. It will mainly include time and cost considerations. Any course of action requires company specific considerations and should be determined most specifically to demonstrate to the US federal government a "good-faith" effort.

Intelligence Cycle Approach for the POAM Lifecycle

This chapter is designed to provide a structure for anyone developing a POAM for its company or agency. It describes how to approach the POAM development process and how to easily formulate and track POAMs during their lifecycle. We suggest using the US Intelligence Community's *Intelligence Cycle* as a guide to handle POAM's from "cradle-to-grave." The process has been slightly modified to provide a more pertinent description for the purposes of POAM creation, but we have found this model to be effective for the novice through professional cybersecurity or IT specialist that works regularly in this area.

This includes the following six stages:

1. **IDENTIFY:** Those controls that time, technology or cost that cannot be met to satisfy the unimplemented control.

2. **RESEARCH:** You now have decided the control is not going to meet your immediate NIST needs. The typical initial milestone is to research what it is, how the federal government wants it implemented, and the need to identify the internal challenges the company may face from a people, process, or technology perspective.

3. **RECOMMEND:** At this phase, all research and analysis has been done, and presumably well-documented. Typically, the cybersecurity team or business IT team will formulate recommended solutions to the System Owner, i.e., the business decision-makers such as the Chief Information or Operations Officer. The recommendations must not only be technically feasible, but cost and resources should be part of any recommendation.

4. **DECIDE:** At this point, company decision-makers not only approve of the approach to correct the security shortfall but have agreed to resourcing requirements to authorize the expenditures of funds and efforts.

5. **IMPLEMENT:** Finally, the solution is implemented, and the POAM is updated for closure. This should be reported to the Contract Office or its representative on a recurring basis.

6. **CONTINUAL IMPROVEMENT.** Like any process, it should be regularly reviewed and updated specific to the needs and capabilities of the company or organization. This could include better templates, additional staffing, or more regular updates to management to ensure both a thorough but supportive understanding of how cybersecurity meets the needs and mission of the business.

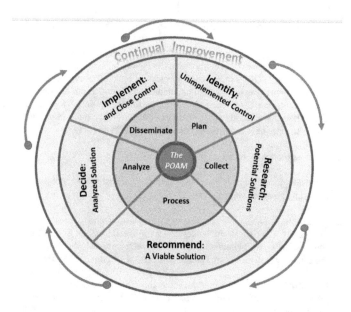

The POAM Lifecycle

We begin in the "Identify" section of the lifecycle process. At this stage several things may occur. The business owner or IT staff recognizes that the security control is not or cannot be immediately met, or they employ automated security tools, such as ACAS® or Nessus®, that identifies securities vulnerabilities within the Information System. This could also include finding that default passwords, like "PASSWORD" have not been changed on internal switches or routers. It could also include the scans have discovered that updated security patching has not occurred; some automated systems will not only identify but recommend courses of action to mitigate or fix a security finding. Always try to leverage these tools as soon as possible to secure an IT environment.

Mitigations must be based upon a strategy that is specific and addresses the risk. The risk may be broad such as widely known risks. Such risks may be found using open-source information threat sources and databases about nation-state actors. It can also be found using automated tools, for example, that identify weaknesses created by not applying security patches to an Operating System or application.

While the objective is to develop a well-written POAM, it should always be based upon a specific risk. Sometimes this may not be possible based upon, for example, the federal government's restriction for sharing "classified" information about a certain risk or threat. The mitigation should be commensurate (and preferably, overwhelming) toward the threat. Mitigating approaches, for example, the technical addition of better malware tools, stronger physical security controls of a site, or even better training of personnel, should always be a consideration in formulating an interim solution (milestone) that reduces the threat, but recognize is may not necessarily eliminate it.

Furthermore, **technical mitigations,** such as security hardware or software additions, should be about reducing the attack surfaces, impacts, or likelihoods of a successful exploit attempt. These should never be relied upon in total, and should consider improvements in company or agency processes, procedures, and personnel practices.

Also, assumed in this stage is the act of documenting findings. The finding should be placed in a POAM template as the business or agency moves through the lifecycle. This could be done using documents created in Word®, for example, but the better recommendation is using a spreadsheet program that allows the easier filtering and management of the POAM. Spreadsheets afford greater flexibility during the "heavy lift" portion of formulating all POAM's not intended to be fixed immediately. These may be because of technical shortfalls ("don't have in-house technical expertise to setup Two Factor Authentication (2FA)") or because of financial limitations ("the costs are currently prohibitive to implement the controls as required.")

In the "research" phase this includes technical analyses, Internet searches, market research, etc., regarding viable solutions to address the security control not being "compliant." This activity is typically part of initial milestone established in the POAM. It should be added in the POAM, and could be, for example: "Conduct an initial market research of candidate systems that can provide an affordable Two Factor Authentication (2FA) solution to meet security control 3.X.X." Another example might be: "The cybersecurity section will identify at least two candidate Data at Rest (DAR) solutions to protect the company's corporate and CUI data." These initial efforts are a normal part of any initial milestones that clearly describe reasonable actions to address non-compliant controls.

Another part of any milestone establishment action is to identify when the milestone will be complete. Typically, milestones are done in increments of every 30-days. If the complexity of such an activity requires additional time, ensure the company has identified reasonable periods of times with actual dates of *expected* completion; never use undefined milestones such as "next version update" or "Calendar Year 2020 in Quarter 4." Real dates are mandatory to truly manage findings supported by automated workflow or tracking applications of expiring or expired POAMs.

At the "recommendation" phase, this is the time when the prior research has resulted in at least one solution, be it additional skilled personnel (people), enhanced company policies that manage the security control better (process), or a device that solves the control in part or total (technology). This should be part of this phase and be included in the POAM template as a milestone with the EXPECTED completion date.

At the "decide" phase, company or agency decision-makers should approve a recommended solution. The decision should be documented in a configuration change tracking document, configuration management decision memorandum or in the POAM itself. This should include approved resources, but most importantly, any funding decision should be acted upon as quickly as possible. While many of these suggestions may seem basic, it is often overlooked to document the decision so future personnel and management can understand how the solution was determined.

The "implementation" phase may become the most difficult. It is where a lead should be designated to coordinate the specific activity to meet the control— it may not necessarily be a technical solution and could be a documentation development activity that creates a process to manage the POAM.

Implementation should also include basic programmatic considerations. This should include performance, schedule, cost, and risk:

- Performance: consider what success the solution is attempting to address. Will it have the ability to send email alerts to users? Will the system shutdown automatically once an intrusion is confirmed into the corporate network? Will the Incident Response Plan include notifications to law enforcement? Performance is always a significant and measureable means to ensure that the solution will address the particular POAM shortfall. Always try to measure performance specific to the actual control is being met.

- Schedule: Devise a plan based upon the developed milestones as reasonable and not unrealistic. As soon as a deviation becomes apparent, ensure that the POAM template is updated and approved by management who has the authority to provide extensions to the current plan. This could include, for example, the Senior IT Manager, Chief Information Security Officer, or Chief Operating Officer.

- Cost: While it is assumed all funding has been provided early in the process, always ensure contingencies are in place to request additional funding. It is common in most IT programs to maintain a 15-20% funding reserve for emergencies. Otherwise, the Project Manager or lead will have to re-justify to management for additional funding late in the implementation portion of the cycle.

- Risk: This is not the risk identified, for example, by the review of security controls or automated scans of the system. This risk is specific to the program's success to accomplish its goal to close the security finding.

Risk should always in particular focus on the performance, cost, and schedule risks as major concerns. Consider creating a risk matrix or risk log to help during the implementation phase.

Finally, ensure that as soon as the company or agency can satisfactorily implement its solution, close the control and notify the appropriate office to include, for example, the System Owner, Authorizing Official or Contract Office of the completion.

A concluding area to consider in terms of best-practices within cybersecurity, and more specifically in developing complete POAMs, is the area of continual improvement. Leveraging the legacy Intelligence Lifecycle process should be a good example for IT and cybersecurity specialists to emulate. Everyone supporting this process should always be prepared to make changes or modifications that better represent the state and readiness of the system with its particular listing of POAMs.

For the technically-capable company:
Consider importing POAM spreadsheets into a database program and using its internal automated reporting capabilities. It can be used to enhance POAM status reporting and tracking for Senior Management.

POAM Template

There are two approaches to organizing an Information System's POAM. The less preferred approach is using a document or memorandum assembly of all active POAMs. The difficulty with this approach it is cumbersome and is very difficult to track the status of current and pending POAMs in an efficient manner. The typical approach is using a spreadsheet because it lends itself to "tailoring" to provide recurring and ad hoc reports to the IT staff and company leadership. Especially important is its ability to filter columns and present a current picture of the state of POAMs.

The key four elements of any POAM are the: 1) finding, vulnerability or weakness identified; 2) the milestones, whether they are accomplished and reviewed monthly or quarterly; 3) resources or who and what are focused on attaining a compliant control; and, 4) the expected completion date; this last component is the most critical. *A POAM is considered incomplete if this element is not addressed with an actual calendar date.*

Other factors that assist in managing the control's completion is the specific control affected, for example "Control 3.3.4," any unique identifiers, for example, a "security patch is missing for Adobe Pro® 9.2.5," or a Common Vulnerabilities Exposure (CVE) identifier. (See https://cve.mitre.org/ for current open source vulnerability findings captured and categorized by the MITRE® Corporation).

Elements of an Effective POAM
1. Identified Vulnerability or Weakness (tied to a security control)
2. Milestones (monthly, quarterly)
3. Resources (people, process, and technology)
4. Expected Completion end-date

POAMs must include all known security weaknesses within the Information System and should use a POAM template as found below. The POAM template should be as complete as possible and should at a minimum address the four *elements* identified.

The Template

The following "agile" template was created with the requisite number of effective categories(columns) to adequately meet the requirements of NIST 800-171. While more columns may be added by the user for a more detailed view, this version was designed with the basic standard categories found in many parts of the DOD and federal government within its cybersecurity system development and assessment teams.

The POAM template, when completed, should be marked "Controlled Unclassified Information (CUI)" as a banner across the top. If you are working with DOD, you most likely will also be required to add the "Critical Defense Information (CDI)" banner as well.

CONTROLLED UNCLASSIFIED INFORMATION/CRITICAL DEFENSE INFORMATION (DOD ONLY) – [WHEN FILLED IN]

Plan of Action & Milestones *Template

SYSTEM NAME:

System Information:

System Name	
Company/Organization	
Sponsoring Service/Agency	

POAM History:

Date of this POAM	
Date of Last Update	
Date of Original POAM	

POAM Contact Information:

POC Name/Title	
POC Phone	
POC Email	

Security Costs (optional):

Security Costs (TOTAL):	
Personnel	
Equipment	

*ADD ADDITIONAL COLUMNS for MILESTONE ACTIVITY & COMPLETION DATE AS NEEDED

(1) Status (G, Y, R)	(2) NIST 800- 171 Control Family	(3) NIST 800- 171 Identifier	(4) Scan Identifier	(5) Weakness/ Deficiency Identifier	(6) Weakness or Deficiency	(7) POC	(8) Resources Required	(9) Overall Completion Date	(10A) Milestone Activity	(10B) Milestone Completion Date-1	(10C) Milestone Activity	(10D) Milestone Completion Date-3	(10E) Milestone Activity	(10F) Milestone Completion Date-3	(11) Changes to Milestone	(12) Risk Level High/Moderate /low High	(13) Estimated Sec. Cost	(14) Comments
*NONE Compliant Controls to next tab>																		
G	AC	3.1.8		System Administrator	No limits on unsuccessful logon	Susan James	None	1-Jun-19	Set policy setting to forced lockout of users failing 3 logon	1-Jun-19						Low		0 Policy setting update required by authorized privileged user
Y	AT	3.2.3		COO	No assigned insider threat security officer	Alice Cooper	Additional budget for one full-time security person	15-Jun-19	Job announcement out on	15-Apr-19	Begin interviews	15-May-19	Select/begin new insider threat	15-Jun-19		Med	$80,000	Hiring action approved by President 10-Jun
R		CVE-1234	ACAS	Elbow Bleed Patch missing	John Smith	Patch computers activated	20-Apr-19	Test patch in tested environment ABCD3	20-Apr-19	Deploy Patch to 200 servers globally	20-Apr-19			None		Med		#IT testing patch with roll back standard IT procedures
	IA	3.5.3		System Administrator	Not using multifactor authentication for local and network access	Bob Dole	Equipment, servers, IA consultant tokens for all employees	20-Oct-19	Conduct research on solutions	15-Jun-19	Recommend to leadership	15-Jun-19	Begin/complete install of all equipment	4-Jun-19	20-Oct-19 *Potential if training cannot assist and create classroom instruction, etc.	High	$265,000	May require POAM extension of all PPT components not in place by 20 Oct 2019

NIST-Based POAM Template (2018)

Template Instructions

1. <u>SYSTEM NAME:</u> This should be the name recorded as the network or system used to identify it for the purposes of company funding or budget line. It may be described as, for example, the "Company ABC's Enterprise Network," or "Managed Services Corporate IT Infrastructure."

2. <u>System Information</u>

   a. <u>System Name.</u> The system name may be repeated here.
   b. <u>Company/Organization Name.</u> The company who owns and provides funding for the care and maintenance of the overall IT system.
   c. <u>Sponsoring/Service Agency</u>. This would be the major federal agency that the company is supporting such as the Department of Health and Human Services, or if a subcontractor to another prime contractor it would be identified by that company's name such as the "Really Big Company."

3. <u>POAM Contact Information</u>

   a. <u>POC/Name Title</u>. This would typically be someone on the IT staff or the designated Information System Security Officer (ISSO) responsible for maintaining the record of the system to include the SSP or POAM listing.
   b. <u>POC Phone</u>. This should be their work and mobile number to contact.
   c. <u>POC Email.</u> This should be their company email address.

4. <u>POAM History</u>

   a. <u>Date of this POAM.</u> The date of the current for-record POAM that may be inspected at any time by the Contract Office or their designated representative.
   b. <u>Date of last Update.</u> The date when last updated before the current date of the POAM in 4.a.
   c. <u>Date of Original POAM</u>. This should have been the first version of the POAM submitted for review and approval.

5. <u>Security Costs (optional):</u> This area is designed as optional. Federal agencies are required to identify overall cybersecurity costs of all expenditures. This could include computer products, services, equipment, personnel cost, and training, etc. It is suggested that the company attempt to identify all costs to manage its IT infrastructure and all associated cybersecurity activities.
   a. Security Costs (TOTAL)
   b. Personnel
   c. Equipment

There are multiple categories specific to the specific NIST framework that should be maintained to prepare a complete POAM. Companies may increase the number of categories to provide additional visibility and tracking capabilities. For the purposes of this standard POAM, the intent is to provide the absolute minimum number of controls to manage the POAM template during the life of the IT system or environment.

1. Status: This should be a company defined status of the progress toward completion. Suggested approaches can be either quantitative or qualitative and may include:
   a. GREEN: 100% or excellent
   b. YELLOW: >50% and <100% or good to very good
   c. RED: <50% or fair to poor

2. Control Family: This should be the NIST family, for example, Access Control (AC), Configuration Management (CM), etc.

3. Identifier: This will align with the NIST numeric system, for example, 3.1.2, 3.10.4, etc.

4. Scan Identifier: This category will be used when a manual or automated scan identifies within the system a specific finding. These systems provide a finding identifier unique to the approach or automated tool. Examples include Nessus® or other automated tool and its unique serialization.

5. Weakness or Deficiency Identified by: This should the individual who identifies the weakness. This could be a developer, auditor, etc. This block should also include any guidance or tool that had identified the current weakness or deficiency.

6. Weakness or Deficiency: This is the specific finding. This could include, for example:
   a. Control 3.1.1 is not compliant.... A short description of that control would be appropriate.
   b. "Jojo 2.3" security patch is missing. Current version is "Jojo 1.9."

7. Point of Contact (POC): This should be the responsible individual who will manage this POAM until closure. This may be IT staff members, ISSO, etc.

8. Resources Required: This should identify what is needed to close this finding. What are the people, process (time to develop), and technology (additional hardware or software) items needed? Costs should be captured under the "Estimated Cost" category.

9. Overall Completion Date: This is the most important column. This should be the planned and expected physical date when the POAM will be closed.

10. Milestones (multiple): This column may need to be replicated as much as needed. Milestones could be monthly or quarterly based on the direction from the agency or Contract Office.

    a. Actions: These are the activities that lead to POAM completion. See the section, **Intelligence Cycle Approach for the POAM Lifecycle.**

    b. Expected milestone date: This should be a calendar date.

11. Changes to Milestones: This column should capture any deviations from the POAM, approvals from the business, and any miscellaneous information that may adversely impact the POAM's management.

12. Risk Level: The federal government has yet to "security categorize" vulnerabilities that occur based upon a partial or incomplete interpretation of, for example, NIST 800-171. Businesses using some automated tools most likely will abide by the US DOD's categorization under NIST 800-53 revision 4 and other cybersecurity documents. For the current use of this POAM template suggested interpretations are offered; predominantly based on the DOD's security categorization model.

    a. High (Category 1): If the agency has issued, for example, directed policy, such as Two-factor Authentication as a requirement, this control should be marked as "High."

    b. Moderate (Category 2): For example, if the business has an unmet **technical control**; a control requiring some form of technical solution, such as automated auditing, this should be considered at a minimum as a "moderate" risk.

    c. Low (Category 3): Controls that require some form of **documentation-based control**, such as the Incident Response Plan (IRP) or Continuous Monitoring Plan (CMP) should be identified as "low."

13. Estimated Cost: This should be the overall cost to fix the control. This should be an estimated dollar value and updated as better information is received.

14. Comments: Any general comments should be included here about the progress of meeting the specified control.

Conclusion

The POAM is a critical part of any active risk management process, and more importantly, it is a vital activity for any company, business, or agency seeking to provide products or services to the US government. With the new and growing demands for companies to get their "house in order," and to meet cybersecurity readiness the implications are far reaching. This book is designed with providing important information on how to think about and prosecute a successful POAM.

The objective is to provide business owners and their IT staff more practical and in-depth information to meet the contractual requirements currently mandated. The POAM supplement, as well as the System Security Plan (SSP) supplement," was developed to make the process more easily addressed.

This supplement was not just about protecting the sensitive data of the US government, but a means for businesses to protect their Intellectual Property, sensitive data, etc., from loss, compromise or destruction by the varied current threats in cyberspace. POAMs are a critical component of the final BOE submission to the Contract Office. It is vital that the business, with its IT staff, attempt a true good-faith effort that meets those mandates and requirements for the security of their IT systems.

Appendix A – Checklist of Effective Mitigation Development

A mitigation statement should always identify the mitigation factors (people, processes, and technologies) that DIRECTLY addresses the reduction of a risk of a vulnerability for an open finding—either as an incomplete security control implementation, missing patches, or hardware device not properly security configured.

A good mitigation statement for a POAM:

_____ Be concise in the description; no more than 3 full sentences that describes "how" the mitigation(s) used reduced the risk/threat.

TYPES OF MITIGATIONS:
_____ PEOPLE:
    EXAMPLES: Increased training; more specialized personnel, etc.
_____ PROCESS
    EXAMPLES: New procedures; new workflows, etc.
_____ TECHNOLOGY
    EXAMPLES: Operating Systems (different, upgraded), applications, automated tools, IT Hardware solutions, etc.

_____ Address both the implications to the local system (within the company facility) and remote (other locations and, specifically, interfaces with federal government IT assets/systems/networks.

_____ Should NOT differentiate between privileged and non-privileged users; the assumption is that the vulnerability is exploitable by inside/outside threats that have illegally obtained elevated security credentials.

_____ Address how the mitigation(s) have reduced the impact(s) of the existing vulnerability.

_____ Identify a specific source recommendation. (Many automated scanning tools will provide courses of action to employ to address the vulnerability such as update patches and potential "workarounds."

DO NOT

___ ...Rationalize why the vulnerability cannot be addressed.

    ___ Too hard; "We have never have had to do this before"; no threat to system—then why is this a vulnerability?

___ ...Providing information not related to the vulnerability. ("We just upgraded the Operating System", but the vulnerability has to do with, for example, no training program.

___ ...Just describing the background checks and clearance level of personnel. (Remember Mr. Snowden).

Appendix B—Relevant References

Federal Information Security Modernization Act of 2014 (P.L. 113-283), December 2014.
http://www.gpo.gov/fdsys/pkg/PLAW-113publ283/pdf/PLAW-113publ283.pdf

Executive Order 13556, *Controlled Unclassified Information*, November 2010.
http://www.gpo.gov/fdsys/pkg/FR-2010-11-09/pdf/2010-28360.pdf

Executive Order 13636, *Improving Critical Infrastructure Cybersecurity*, February 2013.
http://www.gpo.gov/fdsys/pkg/FR-2013-02-19/pdf/2013-03915.pdf

National Institute of Standards and Technology Federal Information Processing Standards
Publication 200 (as amended), *Minimum Security Requirements for Federal Information
and Information Systems*.
http://csrc.nist.gov/publications/fips/fips200/FIPS-200-final-march.pdf

National Institute of Standards and Technology Special Publication 800-53 (as amended),
Security and Privacy Controls for Federal Information Systems and Organizations.
http://dx.doi.org/10.6028/NIST.SP.800-53r4

National Institute of Standards and Technology Special Publication 800-171, rev. 1,
*Protecting Controlled Unclassified Information in Nonfederal Information Systems and
Organizations.* https://nvlpubs.nist.gov/nistpubs/SpecialPublications/NIST.SP.800-171r1.pdf

National Institute of Standards and Technology Special Publication 800-171A, *Assessing Security
Requirements for Controlled Unclassified Information*
https://csrc.nist.gov/CSRC/media/Publications/sp/800-171a/draft/sp800-171A-draft.pdf

National Institute of Standards and Technology *Framework for Improving Critical
Infrastructure Cybersecurity* (as amended).
http://www.nist.gov/cyberframework

Appendix C—Relevant Terms & Glossary

Audit log.	A chronological record of information system activities, including records of system accesses and operations performed in a given period.
Authentication.	Verifying the identity of a user, process, or device, often as a prerequisite to allowing access to resources in an information system.
Availability.	Ensuring timely and reliable access to and use of information.
Baseline Configuration.	A documented set of specifications for an information system, or a configuration item within a system, that has been formally reviewed and agreed on at a given point in time, and which can be changed only through change control procedures.
Blacklisting.	The process used to identify: (i) software programs that are not authorized to execute on an information system; or (ii) prohibited websites.
Confidentiality.	Preserving authorized restrictions on information access and disclosure, including means for protecting personal privacy and proprietary information.
Configuration Management.	A collection of activities focused on establishing and maintaining the integrity of information technology products and information systems, through control of processes for initializing, changing, and monitoring the configurations of those products and systems throughout the system development life cycle.
Controlled Unclassified Information (CUI).	Information that law, regulation, or governmentwide policy requires to have safeguarding or disseminating controls, excluding information that is classified under Executive Order 13526, Classified National Security Information, December 29, 2009, or any predecessor or successor order, or the Atomic Energy Act of 1954, as amended.
External network.	A network not controlled by a company.

FIPS-validated cryptography. A cryptographic module validated by the Cryptographic Module Validation Program (CMVP) to meet requirements specified in FIPS Publication 140-2 (as amended). As a prerequisite to CMVP validation, the cryptographic module is required to employ a cryptographic algorithm implementation that has successfully passed validation testing by the Cryptographic Algorithm Validation Program (CAVP).

Hardware. The physical components of an information system.

Incident. An occurrence that actually or potentially jeopardizes the confidentiality, integrity, or availability of an information system or the information the system processes, stores, or transmits or that constitutes a violation or imminent threat of violation of security policies, security procedures, or acceptable use policies.

Information Security. The protection of information and information systems from unauthorized access, use, disclosure, disruption, modification, or destruction to provide confidentiality, integrity, and availability.

Information System. A discrete set of information resources organized for the collection, processing, maintenance, use, sharing, dissemination, or disposition of information.

Information Technology. Any equipment or interconnected system or subsystem of equipment that is used in the automatic acquisition, storage, manipulation, management, movement, control, display, switching, interchange, transmission, or reception of data or information by the executive agency. It includes computers, ancillary equipment, software, firmware, and similar procedures, services (including support services), and related resources.

Integrity. Guarding against improper information modification or destruction and includes ensuring information non-repudiation and authenticity.

Internal Network. A network where: (i) the establishment, maintenance, and provisioning of security controls are under the direct control of organizational employees or contractors; or (ii) cryptographic encapsulation or similar security technology implemented between organization-controlled endpoints, provides the same effect (at least about confidentiality and integrity).

Malicious Code. Software intended to perform an unauthorized process that will have adverse impact on the confidentiality, integrity, or availability of an information system. A virus, worm, Trojan horse, or other code-based entity that infects a host. Spyware and some forms of adware are also examples of malicious code.

Media. Physical devices or writing surfaces including, but not limited to, magnetic tapes, optical disks, magnetic disks, and printouts (but not including display media) onto which information is recorded, stored, or printed within an information system.

Mobile Code. Software programs or parts of programs obtained from remote information systems, transmitted across a network, and executed on a local information system without explicit installation or execution by the recipient.

Mobile device. A portable computing device that: (i) has a small form factor such that it can easily be carried by a single individual; (ii) is designed to operate without a physical connection (e.g., wirelessly transmit or receive information); (iii) possesses local, nonremovable or removable data storage; and (iv) includes a self-contained power source. Mobile devices may also include voice communication capabilities, on-board sensors that allow the devices to capture information, and/or built-in features for synchronizing local data with remote locations. Examples include smartphones, tablets, and E-readers.

Multifactor Authentication. Authentication using two or more different factors to achieve authentication. Factors include: (i) something you know (e.g., password/PIN); (ii) something you have (e.g., cryptographic identification device, token); or (iii) something you are (e.g., biometric).

Nonfederal Information System. An information system that does not meet the criteria for a federal information system. nonfederal organization.

Network. Information system(s) implemented with a collection of interconnected components. Such components may include routers, hubs, cabling, telecommunications controllers, key distribution centers, and technical control devices.

Portable storage device. An information system component that can be inserted into and removed from an information system, and that is used to store data or information (e.g., text, video, audio, and/or image data). Such components are typically implemented on magnetic, optical, or solid-state devices (e.g., floppy disks, compact/digital video disks, flash/thumb drives, external hard disk drives, and flash memory cards/drives that contain nonvolatile memory).

Privileged Account User. An information system account with authorizations of a privileged

Privileged User. A user that is authorized (and therefore, trusted) to perform security-relevant functions that ordinary users are not authorized to perform.

Remote Access. Access to an organizational information system by a user (or a process acting on behalf of a user) communicating through an external network (e.g., the Internet).

Risk. A measure of the extent to which an entity is threatened by a potential circumstance or event, and typically a function of: (i) the adverse impacts that would arise if the circumstance or event occurs; and (ii) the likelihood of occurrence. Information system-related security risks are those risks that arise from the loss of confidentiality, integrity, or availability of information or information systems and reflect the potential adverse impacts to organizational operations (including mission, functions, image, or reputation), organizational assets, individuals, other organizations, and the Nation.

Sanitization. Actions taken to render data written on media unrecoverable by both ordinary and, for some forms of sanitization, extraordinary means. Process to remove information from media such that data recovery is not possible. It includes removing all classified labels, markings, and activity logs.

Security Control. A safeguard or countermeasure prescribed for an information system or an organization designed to protect the confidentiality, integrity, and availability of its information and to meet a set of defined security requirements.

Security Control Assessment. The testing or evaluation of security controls to determine the extent to which the controls are implemented correctly, operating as intended, and producing the desired outcome with respect to meeting the security requirements for an information system or organization.

Security Functions.   The hardware, software, and/or firmware of the information system responsible for enforcing the system security policy and supporting the isolation of code and data on which the protection is based.

Threat.   Any circumstance or event with the potential to adversely impact organizational operations (including mission, functions, image, or reputation), organizational assets, individuals, other organizations, or the Nation through an information system via unauthorized access, destruction, disclosure, modification of information, and/or denial of service.

Whitelisting.   The process used to identify: (i) software programs that are authorized to execute on an information system.

"Continuous Monitoring (ConMon): A More Detailed Discussion"

Cybersecurity is not about shortcuts. There are no easy solutions to years of leaders demurring their responsibility to address the growing threats in cyberspace. We hoped that the Office of Personnel Management (OPM) breach several years ago would herald the needed focus, energy and funding to quash the bad-guys. That has proven an empty hope where leaders have abrogated their responsibility to lead in cyberspace. The "holy grail" solution of Continuous Monitoring (ConMon) has been the most misunderstood solution where too many shortcuts are perpetrated by numerous State agencies and the private sector to create an illusion of success. This paper is specifically written to help leaders better understand what constitutes a true statement of: "we have continuous monitoring." This is not about shortcuts. This is about education, training, and understanding at the highest leadership levels that cybersecurity is not a technical issue, but a leadership issue.

The Committee on National Security Systems defines ConMon as: "[t]he processes implemented to maintain current security status for one or more information systems on which the operational mission of the enterprise depends," (CNSS, 2010). ConMon has been described as the holistic solution of end-to-end cybersecurity coverage and the answer to providing an effective global Risk Management (RM) solution. It promises the elimination of the 3-year recertification cycle that has been the bane of cybersecurity professionals.

For ConMon to become a reality for any agency, it must meet the measures and expectations as defined in National Institute of Standards and Technology (NIST) Special Publication (SP) 800-137, Information Security Continuous Monitoring for Federal Information Systems and Organizations. "Continuous monitoring has evolved as a best practice for managing risk on an ongoing basis," (SANS Institute, 2016); it is an instrument that supports effective, continual, and recurring RM assurances. For any agency to truly espouse it has attained full ConMon compliance, it must be able to coordinate all the described major elements as found in NIST SP 800-137.

ConMon is not just the passive visibility pieces, but also includes the active efforts of vulnerability scanning, threat alert, reduction, mitigation, or elimination of a dynamic Information Technology (IT) environment. The Department of Homeland Security (DHS) has couched its approach to ConMon more holistically. Their program to protect government networks is more aptly called: "Continuous Diagnostics and Monitoring" or CDM and includes a need to react to an active network attacker. "The ability to make IT networks, end-points and applications visible; to identify malicious activity; and, to respond [emphasis added] immediately is critical to defending information systems and networks," (Sann, 2016).

Another description of ConMon can be found in NIST's CAESARS Framework Extension: An Enterprise Continuous Monitoring Technical Reference Model (Second Draft). It defines its essential characteristics within the concept of "Continuous Security Monitoring." It is described as a "...risk management approach to Cybersecurity that maintains a picture of an organization's security posture, provides visibility into assets, leverages use of automated data feeds, monitors effectiveness of security controls, and enables prioritization of remedies," (NIST, 2012); it must demonstrate visibility, data feeds, measures of effectiveness and allow for solutions. It provides another description of what should be demonstrated to ensure full ConMon designation under the NIST standard.

The government's Federal Risk and Authorization Management Program (Fed-RAMP) has defined similar ConMon goals. These objectives are all key outcomes of a successful ConMon implementation. Its "... goal[s]...[are] to provide: (i) operational visibility; (ii) annual self-attestations on security control implementations; (iii) managed change control; (iv) and attendance to incident response duties," (GSA, 2012). These objectives, while not explicit to NIST SP 800-37, are well-aligned with the desires of an effective and complete solution.

RMF creates the structure and documentation needs of ConMon; it represents the specific implementation and oversight of Information Security (IS) within an IT environment. It supports the general activity of RM within an agency. (See Figure 1 below). The RMF "... describes a disciplined and structured process that integrates information security and risk management activities into the system development life cycle," (NIST-B, 2011). RMF is the structure that both describes and relies upon ConMon as its risk oversight and effectiveness mechanism between IS and RM.

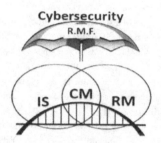

Figure 1. CM "bridges" Information Security and Risk Management

This article provides a conceptual framework to address how an agency would approach identifying a true ConMon solution through NIST SP 800-137. It discusses the additional need to align component requirements with the *"11 Security Automation Domains"* that are necessary to implement true ConMon. (See Figure 2 below). It is through the complete implementation and

Figure 2. The 11 Security Automation Domains (NIST, 2011)

integration with the other described components—See Figure 3 below--that an organization can correctly state it has achieved ConMon.

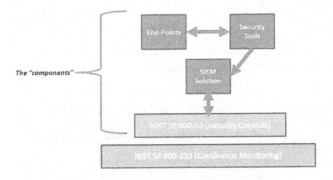

Figure 3. The "Components" of an Effective Continuous Monitoring

Continuous Monitoring – First Generation

For ConMon to be effective and genuine, it must align end-point visibility with security monitoring tools. This includes security monitoring tools with connectivity to "end-points" such as laptops, desktops, servers, routers, firewalls, etc. Additionally, these must work with a highly integrated Security Information and Event Management (SIEM) device. The other "component" is a clear linkage between the end-points, security monitoring tools, and the SIEM appliance, working with the *Security Automation Domains* (See Figure 2). These would include, for example, the areas of malware detection, asset and event management. ConMon must first address these collective components to create a "First Generation" instantiation.

More specifically, a SIEM appliance provides the central core data processing capabilities to effectively coordinate all the inputs and outputs from across the IT enterprise. It manages the data integration and interpretation of all ConMon components. And, it provides the necessary visibility and intelligence for an active incident response capability.

End-point devices must be persistently visible to the applicable security devices. Together, these parts must align with the respective security controls as described in NIST SP 800-53. The selected SIEM tool must be able to accept these inputs and analyze them against defined security policy settings, recurring vulnerability scans, signature-based threats, and heuristic/activity-based analyses to ensure the environment's security posture. The outputs of the SIEM must support the further visibility of the IT environment, conduct and disseminate vital intelligence, and alert leadership to any ongoing or imminent dangers. The expression above is designed to provide a conceptual representation of the cybersecurity professional attempting to ascertain effective ConMon implementation or to develop a complete ConMon answer for an agency or corporation.

Additionally, the SIEM must distribute data feeds in near-real time to analysts and key leaders. It provides for multi-level "dashboard" data streams and issues alert based upon prescribed policy settings. Once these base, First Generation functionalities are consistently aligning with the Security Automation Domains, then an organization or corporation can definitively express it meets the requirements of ConMon.

End-Points

It is necessary to identify hardware and software configuration items that must be known and constantly traceable before implementing ConMon within an enterprise IT environment. End-point visibility is not the hardware devices, but the baseline software of each hardware device on the network.

Configuration Management is also a foundational requirement for any organization's security posture. Soundly implemented Configuration Management must be the basis of any complete CM implementation. At the beginning of any IS effort, cyber-professionals must know the current "as-is" hardware and software component state within the enterprise. End-points must be protected and monitored because they are the most valuable target for would-be hackers and cyber-thieves.

Configuration Management provides the baseline that establishes a means to identify potential compromise between the enterprise's end-points and the requisite security tools. "Organizations with a robust and effective [Configuration Management] process need to consider information security implications concerning the development and operation of information systems including hardware, software, applications, and documentation," (NIST-A, 2011).

The RMF requires the categorization of systems and data as high, moderate, or low regarding risk. The Federal Information Processing Standards (FIPS) Publication 199 methodology is typically used to establish data sensitivity levels in the federal government. FIPS 199 aids the cybersecurity professional in determining data protection standards of both end-points and the data stored in these respective parts. For example, a system that collects and retains sensitive data, such as financial information, requires a greater level of security. It is important that end-points are recognized as repositories of highly valued data to cyber-threats.

Further, cyber-security professionals must be constantly aware of the "...administrative and technological costs of offering a high degree of protection for all federal systems...," (Ross, Katzke, & Toth, 2005). This is not a matter of recognizing the physical end-point alone but the value and associated costs of the virtual data stored, monitored, and protected on a continual basis. FIPS 199 assists system owners in determining whether a higher level of protection is warranted, with higher associated costs, based upon an overall FIPS 199 evaluation.

Security Tools

Security monitoring tools must identify in near-real time an active threat. Examples include anti-virus or anti-malware applications used to monitor network and end-point activities. Products like McAfee and Symantec provide enterprise capabilities that help to identify and reduce threats.

Other security tools would address in whole or part the remaining NIST Security Automation Domains. These would include, for example, tools to provide asset visibility, vulnerability detection, patch management updates, etc. But it is also critical to recognize that even the best current security tools are not necessarily capable of defending against all attacks. New malware or zero-day attacks pose continual challenges to the cybersecurity workforce.

For example, DHS's EINSTEIN system would not have stopped the 2015 Office of Personnel Management breach. Even DHS's latest iteration of EINSTEIN, EINSTEIN 3, an advanced network monitoring and response system designed to protect federal governments' networks, would not have stopped that attack. "...EINSTEIN 3 would not have been able to catch a threat that [had] no known footprints, according to multiple industry experts," (Sternstein, 2015).

Not until there are a much greater integration and availability of cross-cutting intelligence and more capable security tools, can any single security tool ever be fully effective. The need for multiple security monitoring tools that provide "defense in depth" may be a better protective strategy. However, with multiple tools monitoring the same Security Automation Domains, such an approach will certainly increase the costs of maintaining a secure agency or corporate IT environment. A determination of Return on Investment (ROI) balanced against a well-defined threat risk scoring approach is further needed at all levels of the federal and corporate IT workspace.

Security Controls

"Organizations are required to adequately mitigate the risk arising from the use of information and information systems in the execution of missions and business functions," (NIST, 2013). This is accomplished by the selection and implementation of NIST SP 800-53, Revision 4, described security controls. (See Figure 4 below). They are organized into eighteen families to address sub-set security areas such as access control, physical security, incident response, etc. The use of these controls is typically tailored to the security categorization by the respective system owner relying upon FIPS 199 categorization standards. A higher security categorization requires the greater implementation of these controls.

ID	FAMILY	ID	FAMILY
AC	Access Control	MP	Media Protection
AT	Awareness and Training	PE	Physical and Environmental Protection
AU	Audit and Accountability	PL	Planning
CA	Security Assessment and Authorization	PS	Personnel Security
CM	Configuration Management	RA	Risk Assessment
CP	Contingency Planning	SA	System and Services Acquisition
IA	Identification and Authentication	SC	System and Communications Protection
IR	Incident Response	SI	System and Information Integrity
MA	Maintenance	PM	Program Management

**Note that these are all the control families required within DOD. Under the NIST 800-171 effort, not all control families are used or required.

Figure 4. Security Control Identifiers and Family Names, (NIST, 2013)

Security Information and Event Management (SIEM) Solutions

The SIEM tool plays a pivotal role in any viable "First Generation" implementation. Based on NIST and DHS guidance, an effective SIEM appliance must provide the following functionalities:

- "Aggregate data from "across a diverse set" of security tool sources;
- Analyze the multi-source data;
- Engage in explorations of data based on changing needs
- Make quantitative use of data for security (not just reporting) purposes including the development and use of risk scores; and
- Maintain actionable awareness of the changing security situation on a real-time basis," (Levinson, 2011).

"Effectiveness is further enhanced when the output is formatted to provide information that is specific, measurable, actionable, relevant, and timely," (NIST, 2011). The SIEM device is the vital core of a full solution that collects, analyzes, and alerts the cyber-professional of potential and actual dangers in their environment.

There are several major SIEM solutions that can effectively meet the requirements of NIST SP 800-137. They include products, for example, IBM® Security, Splunk®, and Hewlett Packard's® ArcSight® products.

For example, Logrhythm ® was highly rated in the 2014 SIEM evaluation. Logrhythm® provided network event monitoring and alerts of potential security compromises. The implementation of an enterprise-grade SIEM solution is necessary to meet growing cybersecurity requirements for auditing of security logs and capabilities to respond to cyber-incidents. SIEM products will continue to play a critical and evolving role in the demands for "...increased security and rapid response to events throughout the network," (McAfee® Foundstone Professional Services®, 2013). Improvements and upgrades of SIEM tools are critical to providing a more highly responsive capability for future generations of these appliances in the marketplace.

Next Generations

Future generations of ConMon would include specific expanded capabilities and functionalities of the SIEM device. These second generation and beyond evolutions would be more effective solutions in future dynamic and hostile network environments. Such advancements might also include increased access to a greater pool of threat database signature repositories or more expansive heuristics that could identify active anomalies within a target network.

Another futuristic capability might include the use of Artificial Intelligence (AI). Improved capabilities of a SIEM appliance with AI augmentation would further enhance human threat analysis and provide for more automated responsiveness. "The concept of predictive analysis involves using statistical methods and decision tools that analyze current and historical data to make predictions about future events...," (SANS Institute). The next generation would boost human response times and abilities to defend against attacks in a matter of milli-seconds vice hours.

Finally, in describing the next generations of ConMon, it is not only imperative to expand data, informational and intelligence inputs for new and more capable SIEM products, but that input and corresponding data sets must also be fully vetted for completeness and accuracy. Increased access to signature and heuristic activity-based analysis databases would provide greater risk reduction. Greater support from private industry and the Intelligence Community would also be major improvements for Agencies that are constantly struggling against a more-capable and better-resourced threat.

ConMon will not be a reality until vendors and agencies can integrate the right people, processes, and technologies. "Security needs to be positioned as an enabler of the organization—it must take its place alongside human resources, financial resources, sound business processes and strategies, information technology, and intellectual capital as the elements of success for accomplishing the mission," (Caralli, 2004). ConMon is not just a technical solution. It requires capable organizations with trained personnel, creating effective policies and procedures with the requisite technologies to stay ahead of the growing threats in cyberspace.

Figure 6 below provides a graphic depiction of what ConMon components are needed to create a holistic NIST SP 800-137-compliant solution; this demonstrates the First-Generation representation. There are numerous vendors describing that they have the "holy grail" solution, but until they can prove they meet this description in total, it is unlikely they have a complete implementation of a thorough ConMon solution yet.

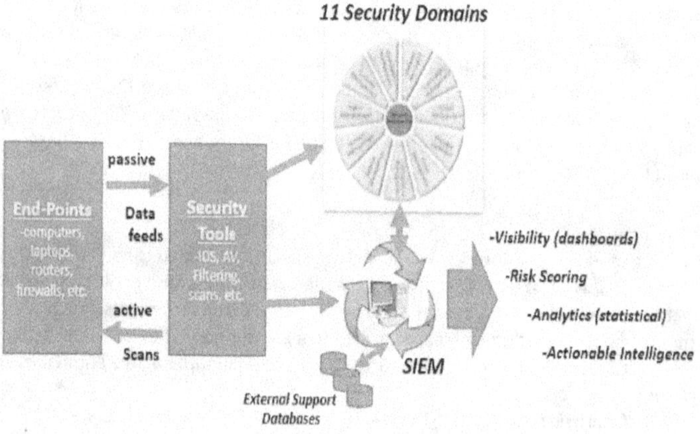

Figure 6. First Generation Continuous Monitoring

Endnotes for "Continuous Monitoring: A More Detailed Discussion"

Balakrishnan, B. (2015, October 6). *Insider Threat Mitigation Guidance* . Retrieved from SANS
 Institute Infosec Reading Room: https://www.sans.org/reading-
 room/whitepapers/monitoring/insider-threat-mitigation-guidance-36307

Caralli, R. A. (2004, December). *Managing Enterprise Security (CMU/SEI-2004-TN-046).*
 Retrieved from Software Engineering Institute:
 http://www.sei.cmu.edu/reports/04tn046.pdf

Committee on National Security Systems. (2010, April 26). *National Information Assurance (IA)
 Glossary.* Retrieved from National Counterintelligence & Security Center:
 http://www.ncsc.gov/nittf/docs/CNSSI-4009_National_Information_Assurance.pdf

Department of Defense. (2014, March 12). *DOD Instructions 8510.01: Risk Management
 Framework (RMF) for DoD Information Technology (IT).* Retrieved from Defense
 Technical Information Center (DTIC):
 http://www.dtic.mil/whs/directives/corres/pdf/851001_2014.pdf

GSA. (2012, January 27). *Continuous Monitoring Strategy & Guide, v1.1.* Retrieved from General
 Services Administration:
 http://www.gsa.gov/graphics/staffoffices/Continuous_Monitoring_Strategy_Guide_072
 712.pdf

Joint Medical Logistics Functional Development Center. (2015). JMLFDC Continuous Monitoring
 Strategy Plan and Procedure. Ft Detrick, MD.

Kavanagh, K. M., Nicolett, M., & Rochford, O. (2014, June 25). *Magic Quadrant for Security
 Information and Event Management.* Retrieved from Gartner:
 http://www.gartner.com/technology/reprints.do?id=1-
 1W8AO4W&ct=140627&st=sb&mkt_tok=3RkMMJWWfF9wsRolsqrJcO%2FhmjTEU5z17u
 8IWa%2B0gYkz2EFye%2BLIHETpodcMTcVkNb%2FYDBceEJhqyQJxPr3FKdANz8JpRhnqAA
 %3D%3D

Kolenko, M. M. (2016, February 18). *SPECIAL-The Human Element of Cybersecurity.* Retrieved
 from Homeland Security Today.US: http://www.hstoday.us/briefings/industry-
 news/single-article/special-the-human-element-of-
 cybersecurity/54008efd46e93863f54db0f7352dde2c.html

Levinson, B. (2011, October). *Federal Cybersecurity Best Practices Study: Information Security
 Continuous Monitoring.* Retrieved from Center for Regulatory Effectiveness:
 http://www.thecre.com/fisma/wp-content/uploads/2011/10/Federal-Cybersecurity-
 Best-Practice.ISCM_2.pdf

McAfee® Foundstone® Professional Services. (2013). *McAfee.* Retrieved from White Paper:
 Creating and Maintaining a SOC: http://www.mcafee.com/us/resources/white-
 papers/foundstone/wp-creating-maintaining-soc.pdf

NIST. (2011-A, August). *NIST SP 800-128: Guide for Security-Focused Configuration
 Management of Information Systems.* Retrieved from NIST Computer Security Resource
 Center: http://csrc.nist.gov/publications/nistpubs/800-128/sp800-128.pdf

NIST. (2011-B, September). *Special Publication 800-137: Information Security Continuous Monitoring (ISCM) for Federal Information Systems and Organizations.* Retrieved from NIST Computer Security Resource Center:
http://csrc.nist.gov/publications/nistpubs/800-137/SP800-137-Final.pdf

NIST. (2012, January). *NIST Interagency Report 7756: CAESARS Framework Extension: An Enterprise Continuous Monitoring Technical Reference Model (Second Draft), .* Retrieved from NIST Computer Resource Security Center:
http://csrc.nist.gov/publications/drafts/nistir-7756/Draft-NISTIR-7756_second-public-draft.pdf

NIST. (2013, April). *NIST SP 800-53, Rev 4: Security and Privacy Controls for Federal Information Systems .* Retrieved from NIST:
http://nvlpubs.nist.gov/nistpubs/SpecialPublications/NIST.SP.800-53r4.pdf

Ross, R., Katzke, S., & Toth, P. (2005, October 17). *The New FISMA Standards and Guidelines Changing the Dynamic of Information Security for the Federal Government.* Retrieved from Information Technology Promotion Agency of Japan:
https://www.ipa.go.jp/files/000015362.pdf

Sann, W. (2016, January 8). *The Key Missing Piece of Your Cyber Strategy? Visibility.* Retrieved from Nextgov: http://www.nextgov.com/technology-news/tech-insider/2016/01/key-missing-element-your-cyber-strategy-visibility/124974/

SANS Institute. (2016, March 6). *Beyond Continuous Monitoring: Threat Modeling for Real-time Response.* Retrieved from SANS Institute: http://www.sans.org/reading-room/whitepapers/analyst/continuous-monitoring-threat-modeling-real-time-response-35185

Sternstein, A. (2015, January 6). *OPM Hackers Skirted Cutting-Edge Intrusion Detection System, Official Says .* Retrieved from Nextgov:
http://www.nextgov.com/cybersecurity/2015/06/opm-hackers-skirted-cutting-edge-interior-intrusion-detection-official-says/114649/

About the Author

Mr. Russo is a former Senior Information Security Engineer within the Department of Defense's (DOD) F-35 Joint Strike Fighter program. He has an extensive background in cybersecurity and is an expert in the Risk Management Framework (RMF) and DOD Instruction 8510.01 which implements RMF throughout the DOD and federal government. He holds both a Certified Information Systems Security Professional (CISSP) certification and a CISSP in information security architecture (ISSAP). He holds a 2017 certification as a Chief Information Security Officer (CISO) from the National Defense University, Washington, DC. He retired from the US Army Reserves in 2012 as the Senior Intelligence Officer.

He is the former CISO at the Department of Education where in 2016 he led the effort to close over 95% of the outstanding US Congressional and Inspector General cybersecurity shortfall weaknesses spanning as far back as five years.

Mr. Russo is the former Senior Cybersecurity Engineer supporting the Joint Medical Logistics Development Functional Center of the Defense Health Agency (DHA) at Fort Detrick, MD. He led a team of engineering and cybersecurity professionals protecting five major Medical Logistics systems supporting over 200 DOD Medical Treatment Facilities around the globe.

Mr. Russo was the Chief Technology Officer at the Small Business Administration (SBA). He led a team of over 100 IT professionals in supporting an intercontinental Enterprise IT infrastructure and security operations spanning 12-time zones; he deployed cutting-edge technologies to enhance SBA's business and information sharing operations supporting the small business community. Mr. Russo was the first-ever Program Executive Officer (PEO)/Senior Program Manager in the Office of Intelligence & Analysis at Headquarters, Department of Homeland Security (DHS), Washington, DC. Mr. Russo was responsible for the development and deployment of secure Information and Intelligence support systems for OI&A to include software applications and systems to enhance the DHS mission. He was responsible for the program management development lifecycle during his tenure at DHS.

He holds a Master of Science from the National Defense University in Government Information Leadership with a concentration in Cybersecurity and a Bachelor of Arts in Political Science with a minor in Russian Studies from Lehigh University. He holds Level III Defense Acquisition certification in Program Management, Information Technology, and Systems Engineering. He has been a member of the DOD Acquisition Corps since 2001.

*He is the author of 2018 cybersecurity publication **"DOD NIST 800-171 Compliance Guidebook",** a decisive and in-depth how-to book on understanding what NIST 800-171 security controls truly mean and how to best address them based upon over 25 years as a security and intelligence professional. He also authored in 2017 the article: **Continuous Monitoring: The Holy Grail of Cybersecurity** was published in "Signals Magazine," the corporate magazine of the Armed Forces Communications and Electronic Association (AFCEA).*

See these books from the author. Available on Amazon...

	**Understanding Your Responsibilities...** By Mark A. Russo CISSP-ISSAP	*The "Flagship" book for a real understanding of NIST 800-171.* *Released in April 2018.*
	**System Security Plan (SSP) Template...** By Mark A. Russo CISSP-ISSAP	A supplement guide to "Understanding." Simple, straight-forward, and easy to use.
	**NIST 800-171: "Beyond DOD": Helping...** By Mark A. Russo CISSP-ISSAP	What do you do if NIST 800-171 is required "beyond DOD"?

www.ingramcontent.com/pod-product-compliance
Lightning Source LLC
LaVergne TN
LVHW010041070326
832903LV00071B/4594